Note to Parents and Teachers

The SCIENCE STARTERS series introduces key science vocabulary to young children while encouraging them to discover and understand the world around them. The series works as a set of graded readers in three levels.

LEVEL 1: BEGINNING TO READ
These books can be read alone or as part of guided or group reading.
Each book has three sections:

• Information pages that introduce new words. These key words appear in bold throughout the book for easy recognition.
• A lively story that recalls this vocabulary and encourages children to use these words when they talk and write.
• A quiz and word search ask children to look back and recall what they have read.

TOO HOT OR TOO COLD? looks at HEAT. Below are some answers and activities relating to the questions on the information spreads that parents, carers, and teachers can use to discuss and develop further ideas and concepts:

p. 7 *Why is it cooler in the shade than in the sun?* If the sun shines on something, it heats it up. But in the shade, the light and heat are blocked by a tree or wall, so it is not so hot.

p. 9 *What animals live in a hot desert?* Camels can live in a desert—they can last for a week without a drink of water. Other desert animals such as snakes, spiders, and foxes hide under the ground during the day and come out at night when it is much cooler.

p. 11 *What warm clothes is this girl wearing?* She is wearing a hat and scarf to keep her head and neck warm, a thick coat to keep her body warm, and boots to keep her feet warm.

p. 13 *What other animals have thick fur like a bison?* Animals that live in cold places, such as seals, bears, wolves, yaks, arctic foxes, and rabbits.

p. 15 *What else can you do to warm up or cool down?* Warm up by wearing thicker clothes, rubbing or blowing on your hands—and by hugging someone! You can cool down by wearing thinner clothes (or taking them off), using a fan, or going for a swim.

p. 19 *What else gives out heat to warm a home?* Electric heaters and log fires. Our bodies give out heat too, so lots of people in a room can warm it up too.

p. 21 *What other foods look different when they have been cooked?* e.g. toasted bread, baked cookies, roast vegetables, barbecued meat, and fried eggs.

p. 23 *When do you see steam at home?* Steam comes from a kettle or pan of boiling water.

ADVISORY TEAM

Educational Consultant
Andrea Bright—Science Coordinator, Trafalgar Junior School

Literacy Consultant
Jackie Holderness—former Principal Lecturer in Primary Education, Westminster Institute, Oxford Brookes University

Series Consultants
Anne Fussell—Early Years Teacher and University Tutor, Westminster Institute, Oxford Brookes University

David Fussell—C.Chem., FRSC

CONTENTS

© Aladdin Books Ltd 2007

Designed and produced by
Aladdin Books Ltd

First published in
the United States in 2007 by
Stargazer Books
c/o The Creative Company
123 South Broad Street
P.O. Box 227
Mankato, Minnesota 56002

Printed in the United States
All rights reserved

Editor: Jim Pipe
Design: Flick, Book Design
and Graphics
Picture Research:
Alexa Brown

Thanks to:
• The pupils of Darell Primary School for
appearing as models in this book.
• Laura Khalil for helping to organize the
photoshoots, and the pupils and teachers of
Trafalgar Junior School and St. Nicholas C.E.
Infant School, for testing the sample books.

Library of Congress Cataloging-in-
Publication Data

Hewitt, Sally, 1949-
  Heat / by Sally Hewitt.
    p. cm. -- (Science starters. Level 1)
  Includes index.
  ISBN 978-1-59604-080-9
  1. Heat--Juvenile literature. 2.Temperature
--Juvenile literature. I. Title. II. Series.

QC256.H479 2006
536--dc22

                              2005056017

Photocredits:
l-left, r-right, b-bottom, t-top,
c-center, m-middle
Front cover tl — Comstock.
Front cover tm — TongRo. Front
cover tr, 17 — Photodisc. Front
cover b, 2ml, 5, 10, 14tr & bl,
16b, 19, 24mr, 25, 26tl & mr,
27 both, 28 both, 29
(foreground), 30 both, 31ml,
32tr, mrt & mr — Marc
Arundale / Select Pictures. 2tl, 6b,
31tr, 32mlt — Stockbyte. 2bl, 8,
12, 15, 18m, 22tr, 23, 24bl, 26b,
29 (background), 31bl, 32mlb,
bl, mrb & br — Corbis. 3, 32ml
— Digital Vision. 4, 20, 21, 32tl
— US Navy. 6t — NASA. 7, 13,
31mr — Corel. 9 —
istockphoto.com. 11 — Digital
Vision. DAJ — 16tr. 18bl —
Ingram Publishing. PBD — 22bl.

HEAT
Too Hot or Too Cold?

by Sally Hewitt

Stargazer Books

What is **hot**?

Fire is **hot**.

It looks **hot**.

It feels **hot**.

Don't get too near.

Fire can burn you!

4

What is **cold**?
Ice cream is **cold**.

It makes your mouth feel **cold**
when you eat it.

• What other things *feel* hot? What *feels* cold?

The **sun** is a great big ball of fire.

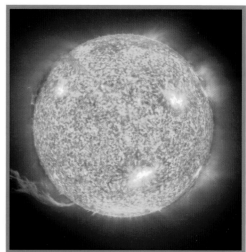

It is very hot!

The **sun** makes you feel hot too. It **heats** our world.

A tree blocks light from the **sun**.

The tree makes a shadow.
It is not so hot in the **shade**.

• Why is it cooler in the shade than in the sun?

At the North Pole it is
always **very cold**.

Snow and ice cover the ground.
Seals and bears live on the ice.

Seal

The sun makes the
desert **very hot**.

The heat dries up all the water.

Camels

• What animals live in a hot desert?

Sun hat   **Sunscreen**

On a hot day,
thin **clothes** keep you **cool**.

The sun can burn your skin,
so wear a sun hat and sunscreen.

On a cold day, thick **clothes** keep you **warm**.

Boots keep your toes **warm** too!

• What warm clothes is this girl wearing?

Bison live in places that
are very cold in winter.

They have thick **fur**
to keep them warm.

12

An elephant lives in hot places.

It has thick **skin.**

This **protects** it from the sun.

It flaps its enormous ears to keep cool.

• What other animals have thick fur like a bison?

Running makes
you feel hot.

Your body
makes little
drops of water
called **sweat**.

Sweat helps to
cool you down.

When your body feels too cold,
you **shiver**.

Shivering helps to warm you up.

- What else can you do to warm up or cool down?

When you are sick you can feel hot and sweaty or cold and shivery.

A thermometer measures how hot you are. This is your **temperature**.

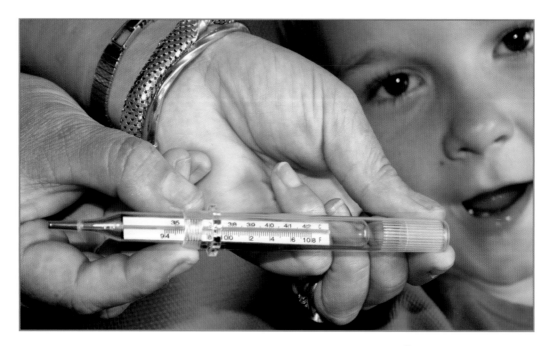

Thermometer

The **temperature** of the air
is how hot or cold it is outside.

Hot air makes you feel warm.
Cool air makes you feel cool.

Lava from a volcano is red-hot.
It **glows** with heat.

A light bulb **glows**
with heat too.

A radiator gives out heat
and keeps your home warm.

A radiator doesn't look hot.
But be careful, it can feel hot!

• What else gives out heat to warm a home?

A refrigerator is cold inside.
It keeps food cold and fresh.

A **freezer** keeps food as cold as ice!
It **freezes** the food.

An oven heats up and gets very hot.
An oven at home **cooks** food.

A cake looks different after
it is **cooked** in a hot oven.

When water is very cold it freezes and changes into **ice**.

When **ice** warms up, it **melts** and changes back into water.

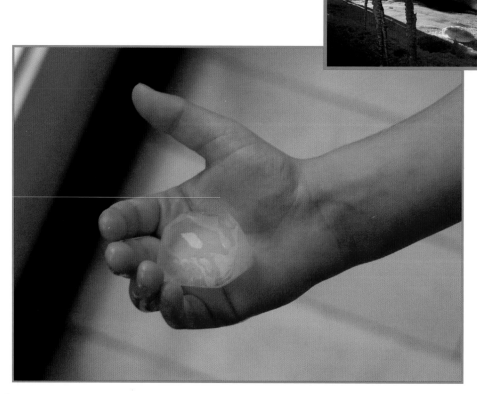

When water is very hot,
it changes into **steam**.

When **steam** cools down,
it changes back into water.

NORTH POLE ADVENTURE

Read the story and look for words about **heat**.

"What are you three up to?" asks Mom.

"We're planning to find the North Pole," says Jared.

"You'll have to wear **warm clothes**," says Mom.

"It's **freezing cold** at the North Pole."

24

Jared, Kate, and Leila try on some **warm** coats. They put on hats, mufflers, mittens, and boots.

"We won't get **cold** at the North Pole now," says Leila.

"It's a sunny day outside," says Mom.

You'll get **hot** and **sweaty** in those clothes."

"It's snowy at the North Pole!" says Jared.

"How will we find the North Pole?" asks Leila.

Mom opens the **freezer**. She takes out some **ice** and puts it in a bowl.

She makes a flag and puts it in the **ice**.

She writes "North Pole" on the flag.

"You'll have to look for it!" she says.

NORTH POLE

Mom hides the North Pole outside.

"Find the North Pole before it **melts**," laughs Mom.

Jared, Kate, and Leila pretend to walk through snow.

They pretend to **shiver** with **cold**.

They look and look for the North Pole.

"I'm **hot!**" says Leila.
"I'm **sweaty!**" says Jared.

"There's the North Pole!" says Kate.
"It's **melted** in the **hot sun!**" says Jared.

The children take off their **warm clothes**.

Mom gives them all an **ice** cream. "These will **cool** you down," she laughs.

Plan an adventure in the desert. What will you wear? What will you take with you?

Draw a picture of you in a **hot**, dry desert.

QUIZ

What **heats** our world?

Answer on page 6

What do you wear on a **hot** day?

Answer on page 10

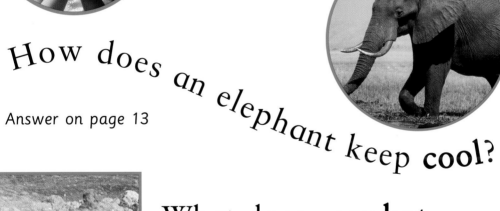

How does an elephant keep **cool**?

Answer on page 13

What does very **hot** water change into?

Answer on page 23

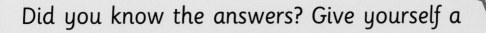

Did you know the answers? Give yourself a

Do you remember these **heat** words?
Well done! Can you remember any more?

 hot
page 4

cold
page 5

 sun
page 6

cool
page 10

 warm
page 11

sweat
page 14

 shiver
page 15

glow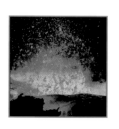
page 18

 ice
page 22

steam
page 23